Yose

the Mari.

A Preliminary Report, 1865

Yosemite and the Mariposa Grove: A Preliminary Report, 1865

Frederick Law Olmsted

Introduction by
Victoria Post Ranney

Illustrated by
Wayne Thiebaud

Foreword by
Dayton Duncan and Ken Burns

Yosemite Association
Yosemite National Park, California

The Yosemite Association is a non-profit, membership
organization dedicated to the support of
Yosemite National Park. Our publishing program is
designed to provide an educational service and to increase
the public's understanding of Yosemite's special qualities
and needs. To learn more about our activities and
other publications, or for information about membership,
please write or call (209) 379-2646.

Library of Congress Cataloging-in-Publication Data

Olmsted, Frederick Law, 1822-1903.
    Yosemite and the Mariposa grove : a preliminary report, 1865 / by
Frederick Law Olmsted ; introduction by Victoria Post Ranney ;
illustrated by Wayne Thiebaud.
      p. cm.
    "First published in Landscape architecture, volume 43, October,
1952"--T. p. verso.
    Includes bibliographical references.
    ISBN 0-939666-68-5 (hard). -- ISBN 0-939666-69-3 (pbk.)
    ISBN-13 978-0939666-69-0
    1. Yosemite Valley (Calif.) -- History. 2. Yosemite National Park
(Calif.) -- History. 3. Landscape architecture -- California -- Yosemite
Valley -- History -- 19th century. I. Title.
F868.Y6046 1993   93-22909
979.4'47 -- dc20   CIP

Yosemite Association
P.O. Box 230
Yosemite National Park, El Portal, CA, 95318

This book was designed by
Michael Osborne Design, modsf.com
The type was set in Monotype Sabon.

FOREWORD

THE NATIONAL PARK IDEA, BORN IN THE United States, is as uniquely American as the Declaration of Independence and just as radical: that a nation's most magnificent and sacred places should be preserved, not for royalty or the rich, but for everyone and for all time. It is, as Wallace Stegner once said, "the best idea we ever had," now copied by other nations around the world.

And it received its first eloquent expression in 1865 in this remarkable and prescient report by Frederick Law Olmsted. No statement since has been so cogent or powerful. Pristine natural landscapes, Olmsted observed, provide people with "refreshing rest and reinvigoration." They are good—perhaps essential—for the soul. Which is why, he noted, that from time immemorial they have most often become the exclusive domain of any society's most privileged classes, "a monopoly, in a very peculiar manner, of a very few, very rich people."

Olmsted believed a great democracy had a greater obligation: "to provide means of protection for all its citizens in the pursuit of happiness." That meant, he argued, that "the establishment by government of great public grounds for the free enjoyment of the people...is thus justified and enforced as a political duty."

Olmsted gave additional reasons for creating public parks, including that they are undeniably good for the local, state, and national economy because of the tourist business they engender. His report also included practical advice about building roads and shelters, as well as instituting regulations to zealously protect the "dignity of the scenery." All of his points are as pertinent today as they were when he first read them to his fellow Yosemite commissioners nearly 150 years ago.

But in deliberately borrowing from our nation's founding document, which proclaims that the "pursuit of happiness" is among the inalienable rights of every human being, and in attaching that notion to why Yosemite (or any other future park) should not be allowed to become "a rich man's park," Olmsted infused the national park idea with its most enduring principle.

Dayton Duncan and Ken Burns
The National Parks: America's Best Idea

INTRODUCTION

IN AUGUST 1865, MEMBERS OF THE FIRST Yosemite Commission camped on the floor of Yosemite Valley and heard their chairman, Frederick Law Olmsted, read the report published here. It was a groundbreaking document, for it laid out reasons justifying the government of a republic in reserving land of scenic value for its people. It also proposed farsighted guidelines for management that still serve as models for administrators and advocates of national parks today.

The previous year, in the depths of the Civil War, Congress had granted Yosemite Valley and the Mariposa Big Tree Grove (the original core of Yosemite National Park) to the State of California. An act signed by President Lincoln on June 30, 1864, transferred the two neighboring sites to California "for public use, resort and recreation" forever.

This unprecedented legislation was the first to set aside one of America's future national parks. Yellowstone, created eight years later in a federal territory where there was no state government to administer it, would be the first national park officially so named. But Yosemite, despite its early years under the jurisdiction of California, was intended from the start as a legacy for the nation. The California Geological Survey's

Yosemite Book proclaimed in 1868 that Yosemite Valley "is an exceptional creation, and as such has been exceptionally provided for both by the Nation and the State – it has been made a National public park and placed under the charge of the State of California."

The act providing for the Yosemite Grant required that the land be managed by the Governor of California and an eight-member commission. On September 28, 1864, Governor Frederick F. Low appointed the Yosemite Commission and placed Olmsted in charge. Olmsted wrote the report which follows on the commission's behalf and addressed it to the California leislature.

It was a fortunate coincidence that Frederick Law Olmsted, architect-in-chief of New York's Central Park, the country's first large urban park, should appear on the California frontier to launch our first national park. In 1863 he had left behind the Union war effort and his work in Central Park and accepted a lucrative position in California. The New York owners of the Mariposa Estate, the largest gold mining operation in the country, had hired him to manage their seventy square-mile property in the western foothills of the Sierra Nevada.

Two hundred miles east of San Francisco, the estate was remote, indeed, from the Mariposa Company board of directors in New York. The transcontinental railroad had not yet been built, and mail took a month to reach California, whether it traveled overland by stagecoach or via sidewheel steamer and the Panama Railroad. The distance so hampered communication that the Mariposa Company board entrusted Olmsted with absolute, unqualified control of the Mariposa Estate. As a friend who visited the estate remarked, "He is a kind of little monarch here."

His empire was dying, however. He quickly discovered that a recent bonanza of the mines had already played out, and that a severe drought impeded mining operations. He began exploring for new veins, and mounted an expedition to find new sources of water. This quest for water took him for the first time into what is now Yosemite National Park.

The chief ore-processing mill on the Mariposa Estate used water from the Merced River, which ran along its northern boundary. In the mountains some thirty miles upstream, the Merced flowed through the wide meadows of Yosemite Valley. Another branch of the river ran past what is now Wawona at the south end of the present national park. Olmsted explored this South Fork to see if he could bring its waters to the estate by a canal. He met Galen Clark, an educated New England frontiersman and future Guardian of the Yosemite Grant, at his camp near where the Wawona Hotel now stands. He also visited the Mariposa Big Tree Grove. The immense, cinnamon-colored sequoias seemed like "distinguished strangers" that "have come down to us from another world," he wrote his wife, who was preparing to join him in California. His fascination with the Yosemite region had begun. "One or two annual trips into it," he told her, "are the highest gratifications peculiar to the country that you have to look forward to."

Olmsted's appearance on the frontier, though a useful coincidence for Yosemite, was quite consistent with the life pattern spun by his multitalented, restless, and demanding character. By the time he reached California at age forty-one, he already had started several careers. Born the son of a prosperous Connecticut merchant in 1822, he decided to become a scientific farmer, but proved unwilling to stay with agriculture for very long. At twenty-one he sailed to China as a seaman on a merchant ship. After a tour abroad in 1850, he wrote *Walks and Talks of an American Farmer in England*, thereby launching a career as a writer.

During the 1850s, as the slavery controversy intensified, Olmsted traveled through the Southern states as a correspondent for the *New York Times*. Anxious to understand the influence of slavery on the South and the nation, he reported on the effects of the slave system on both whites and blacks in various regions: the plantations along the Atlantic seaboard, the Appalachian "back country," and the Texas frontier. His articles, now collected as *The Cotton Kingdom*, remain among our most thoughtful firsthand accounts of slavery.

But Olmsted could not support himself as a writer, and in the summer of 1857 he applied for the position of superintendent of the new Central Park, which recently had been set aside for public use. As an early proponent of the park who was recommended by influential literary friends like Washington Irving, Olmsted landed the job. Thus began his greatest career – as park designer, social and environmental planner, and the father of landscape architecture in America.

Central Park, as Olmsted notes in the beginning of the Yosemite Report, was one of the great artistic achievements of the Civil War. Designed in 1858 by Olmsted and his partner Calvert Vaux, it became an instant success, heavily used by all classes of people. After the war, cities across the country, from Brooklyn to San Francisco and Boston to Louisville, would commission Olmsted to plan their parks. Eventually he designed some seventeen major urban parks, the grounds of the Niagara Reservation and the U.S. Capitol, as well as numerous suburbs, campuses, and private estates.

If the southern journeys brought out Olmsted's observations of the relation between people and their environment, Central Park revealed his extraordinary talent for organization, and his ability to draw up and implement comprehensive plans. He and Vaux laid out separate walking and bridle paths, carriage drives, and sunken crosstown roads that allowed thousands of people to enjoy the park safely together. As architect-in-chief, Olmsted deployed several thousand workers to plant trees and bushes, and build roads, bridges, storm sewers, and lakes. He also organized a force of park keepers, the forerunners of our national park rangers. His detailed instructions cautioned them to behave respectfully toward park visitors, in a manner that would educate as much as control.

When the Civil War broke out, Olmsted became principal administrator of the U.S. Sanitary Commission, which oversaw the health and welfare of the Union soldiers and developed into the largest charitable organization in the history of the country. Two years later, Olmsted's reputation as a manager was such that the New York purchasers of the Mariposa Estate, despite his lack of experience in mining, recruited him to be superintendent of their valuable property on the California frontier.

Olmsted's genius as an executive stemmed from his ability to see the long-range goals of whatever work he took on, and to pursue every detail needed to implement them. He was especially effective in laying the groundwork for new enterprises, like the nation's first major urban park or its first scenic reserve. When the American Freedman's Aid Union was searching for a director to map out its postwar work on behalf of the freed slaves, Henry Whitney Bellows, chairman of the U.S. Sanitary Commission, strongly recommended his former associate, saying,

> Mr. F. L. Olmsted, is, of all men I know, the most comprehensive, thorough & minutely particular organizer. He is equally wonderful in the management of principles & details...If he is willing to take hold tho' only for a *year*, just long eno' to plan your campaign, have him at any *cost*, though you could have any ten others for *nothing*.

The problem with Olmsted, Bellows admitted, was that he did not work well with boards of directors. "They think him impracticable, expensive, slow – when he is only long-headed, with broader, deeper notions of economy than themselves." Although he loved power and was fit to hold it, he did not work well in a team. Furthermore, he was unwilling to compromise his goals for political reasons. At Central Park he had refused to hire for patronage; at the Sanitary Commission he had complained when the commissioners tolerated independent regional branches. At Yosemite the scope and expense of his vision and his failure to take into account the conflicting interests of the other commissioners had unfortunate results for the report.

Because Olmsted tended to think further ahead than his employers, he frequently redefined the task he was appointed to accomplish. His concept for Yosemite, for example, was much broader than that of Congress. He immediately realized that preserving the seven-mile-long Yosemite Valley and the four square miles of the Mariposa Big Tree Grove would not be enough. The mandate of the Yosemite Commission was to manage these two areas only, for that was the extent of the Congressional grant. But Olmsted's report pushes far beyond those boundaries to discuss the surrounding region, most of which has now been incorporated into the national park.

His vision was based on a thorough knowledge of the region, because he had traveled extensively there and had sought the advice of the pioneering scientists and artists at work in the area. In July, 1864, unaware that Congress had just granted the Mariposa Big Tree Grove and Yosemite Valley to California, he mounted an expedition to visit both sites. The pack train which wound through the Sierra forests included Olmsted, his wife Mary, their four young children, an English governess who was an expert on fossils, the geologist William Ashburner and his wife Emilia, and an African-American guide who understood the language of the local Miwok tribes. They stayed several weeks at Clark's Station on the South Fork of the Merced, sharing their campground with a Miwok tribal gathering, and measuring the trunks and cones of the giant sequoias with Galen Clark. Then they moved into Yosemite Valley, where they camped opposite Yosemite Falls.

Later that summer Olmsted explored the High Sierra with his twelve-year-old son John and William Brewer of the California Geological Survey. They rode up above Yosemite Valley through Tuolumne Meadows to Mono Pass on the eastern border of today's national park. There they climbed an unnamed peak and, in the Survey's tradition of honoring eminent scientists, named it for Olmsted's friend Oliver Wolcott Gibbs, whom they considered the foremost chemist in America.

The High Sierra landscape was new to Olmsted's experience. He took note of alpine flowers and high-altitude birds and animals. The bare granite rocks reminded him of "snow-drifts after a very gusty storm, some being of grand simplicity while others are pinnacled, columnar, castleated and fantastic." The wilderness scenery, he wrote his father in Connecticut, was "of a very peculiar character and much the grandest that I have ever seen."

The California Geological Survey's field party was mapping the Sierra Nevada that summer, and Olmsted became friends not only with its leader, William Brewer, but also with the young Clarence King, who later founded the United States Geological Survey. These hardy and well-trained professionals, like the eminent botanist John Torrey, whom he met in the Valley the following year, heightened Olmsted's understanding of the region's extraordinary geology and its rare flora and fauna. They were the models for the scientists that Olmsted would recommend in the Yosemite Report to be members of the commission.

Three young artists – the landscape photographer Carleton Watkins and landscape painters Thomas Hill and Virgil Williams – spent the summer of 1865 in Yosemite Valley. Olmsted valued the ability of artists to publicize the Yosemite Grant, and noted in his report that the photographs of Watkins and the paintings of Albert Bierstadt, who had visited the Valley in 1863, had been instrumental in persuading Congress to pass the Yosemite Grant of 1864. Olmsted enlisted Watkins, Hill and Williams to advise the commission about land-scape. In his report he went further, proposing that four of the eight commissioners be "students of Natural Science or Landscape Artists." In his mind, Yosemite was not only a museum of natural science and native species; it was a field of study for art as well.

Olmsted's own trained eye for landscape is evident in the description of Yosemite scenery he wrote for the California legislators, few of whom had visited the grant. He emphasized that the charm of the Valley lies not in any one feature like the cliffs or waterfalls, but in "the miles of scenery where cliffs of awful height and rocks of vast magnitude and of varied and exquisite col-oring, are banked and fringed and draped and shad-owed by the tender foliage of noble and lovely trees and bushes, reflected from the most placid pools, and associated with the most tranquil meadows, the most playful streams, and every variety of soft and peaceful pastoral beauty."

After describing the scenery of the grant in the report, Olmsted considers the reasons supporting the action of Congress to reserve the area for public purposes. First he cites the economic value of tourism, comparing Yosemite to the Swiss Alps. Then comes his most telling argument, and one novel for his time. He describes the beneficial effect of natural scenery upon the human mind, and claims that a republic owes this benefit to its ordinary citizens.

> If we analyze the operation of scenes of beauty upon the mind, and consider the intimate relation of the mind upon the nervous system and the whole physical economy, the action and reaction which constantly occurs between bodily and mental conditions, the reinvigoration which results from such scenes is readily comprehended.

He argues that British statesmen remain very active into old age because they retreat regularly to their private parks or the mountains. But in America, he believes, this invigorating contact with natural scenery should be available to all citizens. Therefore, it is the duty of a republican government to safeguard its most impressive scenic areas for the use of its citizens.

Olmsted's recommendations to the California legislature for the management of the Yosemite Grant rest on this framework of the purpose of scenic reserves. His first recommendation is preservation: the maintenance of the natural scenery and the restriction of artificial construction, particularly any that would "unnecessarily obscure, distort, or detract from the dignity of the scenery." He had to allow for overnight stays in the Valley, given the time it took to get there from Clark's Station, but he kept structures and facilities to a minimum, and proposed construction of just enough drives and paths to provide access to the scenery without intruding into it.

His second recommendation is public access. Only those travelers who were able to afford a lengthy trip by pack train could visit the Yosemite Valley in Olmsted's day. "As long as the present arrangements continue," he wrote, Yosemite "will remain, practically, the property only of the rich." Improved public access meant constructing a road to the Valley, and Olmsted began to survey the most scenic route.

In his first action as chairman of the Yosemite Commission he had hired Clarence King and his friend James Terry Gardner to survey the boundaries of the grant. As Congress specified, they established the boundary of the Valley one mile back from the precipitous walls, and delineated four square miles to contain the six hundred sequoias of the Mariposa Grove. But Olmsted, thinking beyond the boundaries of the grant, asked Clarence King also to lay out a scenic route between the Valley and the Grove, and from there to the existing roads near the Mariposa Estate. He instructed King to site the road near the most interesting views and the finest forest trees. This road would not only provide access for ordinary citizens and enrich their experience of the scenery; it also would allow the commissioners to bring in supplies from the outside, thus reducing the temptation to cut down the trees and farm the meadows.

Winter storms drove King out of the mountains before he could complete his survey of the road. Much worse, Olmsted's requested appropriation for roads led to the suppression of his report. He asked the state legislature to spend $37,000 for the Yosemite Grant, of which $25,000 was for "aid in the construction of a road," a considerable sum at the time. Nonetheless, the commission adopted his report, according to minutes of the meeting of August 9, 1865, that survive among the Olmsted Papers at the Library of Congress. Olmsted wrote his father on August 28, "We had also a meeting of our Yo Semite Commission, of which I am Chairman, and adopted an elaborate report to the legislature which I had prepared." Five of the eight members of the commission were present, including Olmsted, Galen Clark and William Ashburner.

That November, however, shortly after Olmsted moved back to New York, three members of the Yosemite Commission – Josiah Dwight Whitney, chief of the California Geological Survey, William Ashburner, a former member of the Survey, and Israel Ward Raymond, who had drafted the Yosemite Grant – met in San Francisco. They examined the proposed budget in light of the competing needs of the California Geological Survey, which also was requesting a substantial appropriation from the state in order to complete its work.

The three men, a minority of the Yosemite Commission, then reported to the governor that they had decided unanimously "that it was not expedient, at pre-

sent, to lay the report before the legislature, or to call
for an appropriation so large as $37,000, the sum
demanded by Mr. Olmsted." The report was thus sup-
pressed, never to be submitted to the legislature. Olmsted's farsighted but expensive plans were scuttled in the
interest of political expedience and the State Geological
Survey, by members of his own board, while he moved
on to other endeavors.

Olmsted's ideas were not completely lost to his con-
temporaries, thanks to his good rapport with journal-
ists. In San Francisco he had met a party of influential
public officials and newspapermen who had traveled
across the country, and he scheduled the first meeting of
the Yosemite Commission to coincide with their visit to
the Valley. Carleton Watkins photographed the two parties together on the Valley floor. It is likely the journal-
ists heard Olmsted read his report; certainly they were
familiar with its substance. The Speaker of the U.S.
House of Representatives, Schuyler Colfax, and jour-
nalists from the *New York Tribune*, the *Springfield*
(Massachusetts) *Republican,* the *Chicago Tribune,* and
San Francisco's *Alta California* all returned home to
publicize the Yosemite Grant and the commission's
work.

During the following decades, when California's
administration of Yosemite came under increasing crit-
icism, Olmsted's advice was frequently sought. Though
he hesitated to become involved without current knowledge of the situation, he sent a description of the
Yosemite scenery to the *New York Evening Post* in 1868
as part of a campaign against a bill in Congress that

would have turned over several hundred acres of
Yosemite Valley to settlers claiming land there. Although
he traveled to California to design the Stanford University campus in the 1880s, Olmsted never again visited
Yosemite. He did write a public letter about Yosemite entitled "Governmental Preservation of Natural
Scenery" in March, 1890, shortly before the establishment of Yosemite National Park.

This volume should bring the first report of the
Yosemite Commission the attention it deserves. Olmsted saw the Yosemite region when it was new to all but
Native Americans, and though well over a century has
passed, his description of its landscape gives us a stan-
dard by which to gauge its health today. His analysis of
the restorative effect of natural scenery upon the human
mind still rings true. And park administrators and
advocates who must assure both preservation and public access can take heart from Olmsted's conviction that
this is one of the highest duties a republic can perform
for its people.

Victoria Post Ranney

Editor,
The Papers of Frederick Law Olmsted,
Volume 5: The California Frontier, 1863-1865

YOSEMITE AND
THE MARIPOSA GROVE:
A PRELIMINARY REPORT, 1865

IT IS A FACT OF MUCH SIGNIFICANCE WITH reference to the temper and spirit which ruled the loyal people of the United States during the war of the great rebellion, that a livelier susceptibility to the influence of art was apparent, and greater progress in the manifestations of artistic talent was made, than in any similar period before in the history of the country. The great dome of the Capitol was wholly constructed during the war, and the forces of the insurgents watched it rounding upward to completion for nearly a year before they were forced from their entrenchments on the opposite bank of the Potomac; Crawford's great statue of Liberty was poised upon its summit in the year that President Lincoln proclaimed the emancipation of the slaves. Leutze's frescoe of the peopling of the Pacific States, the finest work of the painter's art in the Capitol; the noble front of the Treasury building with its long colonnade of massive monoliths; the exquisite hall of the Academy of Arts; the great park of New York, and many other works of which the nation may be proud, were brought to completion during the same period. Others were carried steadily on, among them our own Capitol; many more were begun, and it will be hereafter remembered that the first organization formed solely for the cultivation of the fine arts on the Pacific side of the Globe, was established in California while the people of the State were not only meeting the demands of the Government for sustaining its armies in the field but were voluntarily making liberal contributions for binding up the wounds and cheering the spirits of those who were stricken in the battles of liberty.

It was during one of the darkest hours, before Sherman had begun the march upon Atlanta or Grant his terrible movement through the Wilderness, when the paintings of Bierstadt and the photographs of Watkins, both productions of the War time, had given to the people on the Atlantic some idea of the sublimity of the Yo Semite, and of the stateliness of the neighboring Sequoia grove, that consideration was first given to the danger that such scenes might become private property and through the false taste, the caprice or the requirements of some industrial speculation of their holders; their value to posterity be injured. To secure them against this danger Congress passed an act providing that the premises should be segregated from the general domain of the public lands, and devoted forever to popular resort and recreation, under the administration of a Board of Commissioners, to serve without pecuniary compensation, to be appointed by the Executive of the State of California.

His Excellency the Governor in behalf of the State accepted the trust proposed and appointed the required Commissioners; the territory has been surveyed and the Commissioners have in several visits to it, and with much deliberation, endeavored to qualify themselves to present to the Legislature a sufficient description of the property, and well considered advice as to its future management.

The Commissioners have deemed it best to confine their attention during the year which has elapsed since their appointment to this simple duty of preparing themselves to suggest the legislative action proper to be taken, and having completed it, propose to present their resignation, in order to render as easy as possible the pursuance of any policy of management, the adoption of which may be determined by the wisdom of the Legislature. The present report therefore is intended to embody as much as is practicable, the results of the labors of the Commission, which it also terminates.

As few members of the Legislature can have yet visited the ground, a short account of the leading qualities of its scenery may be pardoned.

The main feature of the Yo Semite is best indicated in one word as a chasm. It is a chasm nearly a mile in average width, however, and more than ten miles in length. The central and broader part of this chasm is occupied at the bottom by a series of groves of magnificent trees, and meadows of the most varied, luxuriant and exquisite herbage, through which meanders a broad stream of the clearest water, rippling over a pebbly bottom, and eddying among banks of ferns and rushes; sometimes narrowed into sparkling rapids and sometimes expanding into placid pools which reflect the wondrous heights on either side. The walls of the chasm are generally half a mile, sometimes nearly a mile in height above these meadows, and where most lofty are nearly perpendicular, sometimes overjutting. At frequent intervals, however, they are cleft, broken, terraced and sloped, and in these places, as well as everywhere upon the summit, they are overgrown by thick clusters of trees.

There is nothing strange or exotic in the character of the vegetation; most of the trees and plants, especially those of the meadow and waterside, are closely allied to and are not readily distinguished from those most common in the landscapes of the Eastern States or the midland counties of England. The stream is such a one as Shakespeare delighted in, and brings pleasing reminiscences to the traveller of the Avon or the Upper Thames.

Banks of heartsease and beds of cowslips and daisies are frequent, and thickets of alder, dogwood and willow often fringe the shores. At several points streams of water flow into the chasm, descending at one leap from five hundred to fourteen hundred feet. One small stream falls, in three closely consecutive pitches, a distance of two thousand six hundred feet, which is more than fifteen times the height of the falls of Niagara. In the spray of these falls superb rainbows are seen.

At certain points the walls of rock are ploughed in polished horizontal furrows, at others moraines of boulders and pebbles are found; both evincing the terrific force with which in past ages of the earth's history a glacier has moved down the chasm from among the adjoining peaks of the Sierras. Beyond the lofty walls still loftier mountains rise, some crowned by forests, others in simple rounded cones of light, gray granite. The climate of the region is never dry like that of the lower parts of the state of California; even when, for several months, not a drop of rain has fallen twenty miles to the westward, and the country there is parched, and all vegetation withered, the Yo Semite continues to receive frequent soft showers, and to be dressed throughout in living green.

After midsummer a light, transparent haze generally pervades the atmosphere, giving an indescribable softness and exquisite dreamy charm to the scenery, like that produced by the Indian summer of the East. Clouds gathering at this season upon the snowy peaks which rise within forty miles on each side of the chasm to a height of over twelve thousand feet, sometimes roll down over the cliffs in the afternoon, and, under the influence of the rays of the setting sun, form the most gorgeous and magnificent thunder heads. The average elevation of the ground is greater than that of the highest peak of the White Mountains, or the Alleghenies, and the air is rare and bracing; yet, its temperature is never uncomfortably cool in summer, nor severe in winter.

Flowering shrubs of sweet fragrance and balmy herbs abound in the meadows, and there is everywhere a delicate odor of the prevailing foliage in the pines and cedars. The water of the streams is soft and limpid, as clear as crystal, abounds with trout and, except near its sources, is, during the heat of summer, of an agreeable temperature for bathing. In the lower part of the valley there are copious mineral springs, the water of one of which is regarded by the aboriginal inhabitants as having remarkable curative properties. A basin still exists to which weak and sickly persons were brought for bathing. The water has not been analyzed, but that it possesses highly tonic as well as other medical qualities can be readily seen. In the neighboring mountains there are also springs strongly charged with carbonic acid gas, and said to resemble in taste the Empire Springs of Saratoga.

The other district, associated with this by the act of Congress, consists of four sections of land, about thirty miles distant from it, on which stand in the midst of a forest composed of the usual trees and shrubs of the western slope of the Sierra Nevada, about six hundred mature trees of the giant Sequoia. Among them is one known through numerous paintings and photographs as the Grizzly Giant, which probably is the noblest tree in the world. Besides this, there are hundreds of such beauty and stateliness that, to one who moves among them in the reverent mood to which they so strongly incite the mind, it will not seem strange that intelligent travellers have declared that they would rather have passed by Niagara itself than have missed visiting this grove.

In the region intermediate between the two districts the scenery generally is of grand character, consisting of granite mountains and a forest composed mainly of coniferous trees of great size, yet often more perfect, vigorous and luxuriant than trees of half the size are ever found on the Atlantic side of the continent. It is not, however, in its grandeur or in its forest beauty that the attraction of this intermediate region consists, so much as in the more secluded charms of some of its glens formed by mountain torrents fed from the snow banks of the higher Sierras.

These have worn deep and picturesque channels in the granite rocks, and in the moist shadows of their recesses grow tender plants of rare and peculiar loveliness. The broad parachute-like leaves of the peltate saxifrage, delicate ferns, soft mosses, and the most brilliant lichens abound, and in following up the ravines, cabinet pictures open at every turn, which, while composed of materials mainly new to the artist, constantly recall the most valued sketches of Calame in the Alps and Apennines.

The difference in the elevation of different parts of the district amounts to considerably more than a mile. Owing to this difference and the great variety of exposure and other circumstances, there is a larger number of species of plants within the district than probably can be found within a similar space anywhere else on the continent. Professor Torrey, who has given the received botanical names to several hundred plants of California, states that on the space of a few acres of meadow land he found about three hundred species, and that within sight of the trail usually followed by visitors, at least six hundred may be observed, most of them being small and delicate flowering plants.

By no statement of the elements of the scenery can any idea of that scenery be given, any more than a true impression can be conveyed of a human face by a measured account of its features. It is conceivable that any one or all of the cliffs of the Yosemite might be changed in form and color, without lessening the enjoyment which is now obtained from the scenery. Nor is this enjoyment any more essentially derived from its meadows, its trees, streams, least of all can it be attributed to the cascades. These, indeed, are scarcely to be named among the elements of the scenery. They are mere incidents, of far less consequence any day of the summer than the imperceptible humidity of the atmosphere and the soil. The chasm remains when they are dry, and the scenery may be, and often is, more effective, by reason of some temporary condition of the air, of clouds, of moonlight, or of sunlight through mist or smoke, in the season when the cascades attract the least attention, than when their volume of water is largest and their roar like constant thunder.

There are falls of water elsewhere finer, there are more stupendous rocks, more beetling cliffs, there are deeper and more awful chasms, there may be as beautiful streams, as lovely meadows, there are larger trees. It is in no scene or scenes the charm consists, but in the miles of scenery where cliffs of awful height and rocks of vast magnitude and of varied and exquisite coloring, are banked and fringed and draped and shadowed by the tender foliage of noble and lovely trees and bushes, reflected from the most placid pools, and associated with the most tranquil meadows, the most playful streams, and every variety of soft and peaceful pastoral beauty.

This union of the deepest sublimity with the deepest beauty of nature, not in one feature or another, not in one part or one scene or another, not any landscape that can be framed by itself, but all around and wherever the visitor goes, constitutes the Yo Semite the greatest glory of nature.

No photograph or series of photographs, no paintings ever prepare a visitor so that he is not taken by surprise, for could the scenes be faithfully represented the visitor is affected not only by that upon which his eye is at any moment fixed, but by all that with which on every side it is associated, and of which it is seen only as an inherent part. For the same reason no description, no measurements, no comparisons are of much value. Indeed the attention called by these to points in some definite way remarkable, by fixing the mind on mere matters of wonder or curiosity prevent the true and far more extraordinary character of the scenery from being appreciated.

It is the will of the Nation as embodied in the act of Congress that this scenery shall never be private property, but that like certain defensive points upon our coast it shall be held solely for public purposes.

Two classes of considerations may be assumed to have influenced the action of Congress. The first and less important is the direct and obvious pecuniary advantage which comes to a commonwealth from the fact that it possesses objects which cannot be taken out of its domain that are attractive to travellers and the enjoyment of which is open to all. To illustrate this it is simply necessary to refer to certain cantons of the Republic of Switzerland, a commonwealth of the most industrious and frugal people in Europe. The results of all the ingenuity and labor of this people applied to the resources of wealth which they hold in common with the people of other lands has become of insignificant value compared with that which they derive from the price which travellers gladly pay for being allowed to share with them the enjoyment of the natural scenery of their mountains. These travellers alone have caused hundreds of the best inns in the world to be established and maintained among them, have given the farmers their best and almost the only market they have for their surplus products, have spread a network of rail roads and superb carriage roads, steamboat routes and telegraphic lines over the country, have contributed directly and indirectly for many years the larger part of the state revenues, and all this without the exportation or abstraction from the country of anything of the slightest value to the people.

The Government of the adjoining Kingdom of Bavaria undertook years ago to secure some measure of a similar source of wealth by procuring with large expenditure, artificial objects of attraction to travellers. The most beautiful garden in the natural style on the Continent of Europe was first formed for this purpose, magnificent buildings were erected, renowned artists were drawn by liberal rewards from other countries, and millions of dollars were spent in the purchase of ancient and modern works of art. The attempt thus made to secure by a vast investment of capital the advantages which Switzerland possessed by nature in its natural scenery has been so far successful that a large part if not the greater part of the profits of the Rail Roads, of the agriculture and of the commerce of the kingdom is now derived from the foreigners who have been thus attracted to Munich its capital.

That when it shall have become more accessible the Yosemite will prove an attraction of a similar character and a similar source of wealth to the whole community, not only of California but of the United States, there can be no doubt. It is a significant fact that visitors have already come from Europe expressly to see it, and that a member of the Alpine Club of London having seen it in summer was not content with a single visit but returned again and spent several months in it during the inclement season of the year for the express purpose of enjoying its Winter aspect. Other foreigners and visitors from the Atlantic States have done the same, while as yet no Californian has shown a similar interest it.

The first class of considerations referred to then as likely to have influenced the action of Congress is that of the direct pecuniary advantage to the commonwealth which under proper administration will grow out of the possession of the Yosemite, advantages which, as will hereafter be shown, might easily be lost or greatly restricted without such action.

A more important class of considerations, however, remains to be stated. These are considerations of a political duty of grave importance to which seldom if ever before has proper respect been paid by any Government in the world but the grounds of which rest on the same eternal base, of equity and benevolence with all other duties of a republican government. It is the main duty of government, if it is not the sole duty of government, to provide means of protection for all its citizens in the pursuit of happiness against the obstacles, otherwise insurmountable, which the selfishness of individuals or combinations of individuals is liable to interpose to that pursuit.

It is a scientific fact that the occasional contemplation of natural scenes of an impressive character, particularly if this contemplation occurs in connection with relief from ordinary cares, change of air and change of habits, is favorable to the health and vigor of men and especially to the health and vigor of their intellect beyond any other conditions which can be offered them, that it not only gives pleasure for the time being but increases the subsequent capacity for happiness and the means of securing happiness. The want of such occasional recreation where men and women are habitually pressed by their business or household cares often results in a class of disorders the characteristic quality of which is mental disability, sometimes taking the severe forms of softening of the brain, paralysis, palsey, monomania, or insanity, but more frequently of mental and nervous excitability, moroseness, melancholy, or irascibility, incapacitating the subject for the proper exercise of the intellectual and moral forces.

It is well established that where circumstances favor the use of such means of recreation as have been indicated, the reverse of this is true. For instance, it is a universal custom with the heads of the important departments of the British Government to spend a certain period of every year on their parks and shooting grounds, or in travelling among the Alps or other mountain regions. This custom is followed by the leading lawyers, bankers, merchants and the wealthy classes generally of the Empire, among whom the average period of active business life is much greater than with the most nearly corresponding classes in our own or any other country where the same practice is not equally well established. For instance, Lord Brougham, still an active legislator, is eighty eight years old. Lord Palmerston the Prime Minister is eighty two, Earl Russell, Secretary of Foreign affairs, is 74, and there is a corresponding prolongation of vigor among the men of business of the largest and most trying responsibility in England, as compared with those of our own country, which physicians unite in asserting is due in a very essential part to the habitual cares, and for enjoying reinvigorating recreation.

But in this country at least it is not those who have the most important responsibilities in state affairs or in commerce, who suffer most from lack of recreation; women suffer more than men, and the agricultural class is more largely represented in our insane asylums than the professional, and for this, and other reasons, it is these classes to which the opportunity for such recreation is the greatest blessing.

If we analyze the operation of scenes of beauty upon the mind, and consider the intimate relation of the mind upon the nervous system and the whole physical economy, the action and reaction which constantly occurs between bodily and mental conditions, the reinvigoration which results from such scenes is readily comprehended. Few persons can see such scenery as that of the Yosemite and not be impressed by it in some slight degree. All not alike, all not perhaps consciously, and amongst all who are consciously impressed by it, few can give the least expression to that of which they are conscious. But there can be no doubt that all have this susceptibility, though with some it is much more dull and confused than with others.

The power of scenery to affect men is, in a large way, proportionate to the degree of their civilization and to the degree in which their taste has been cultivated. Among a thousand savages there will be a much smaller number who will show the least sign of being so affected than among a thousand persons taken from a civilized community. This is only one of the many channels in which a similar distinction between civilized and savage men is to be generally observed. The whole body of the susceptibilities of civilized men and with their susceptibilities their powers, are on the whole enlarged. But as with the bodily powers, if one group of muscles is developed by exercise exclusively, and all others neglected, the result is general feebleness, so it is with the mental faculties. And men who exercise those faculties or susceptibilities of the mind which are called in play by beautiful scenery so little that they seem to be inert with them, are either in a diseased condition from excessive devotion of the mind to a limited range of interests, or their whole minds are in a savage state; that is, a state of low development. The latter class need to be drawn out generally; the former need relief from their habitual matters of interest and to be drawn out in those parts of their mental nature which have been habitually left idle and inert.

But there is a special reason why the reinvigoration of those parts which are stirred into conscious activity by natural scenery is more effective upon the general development and health than that of any other, which is this: The severe and excessive exercise of the mind which leads to the greatest fatigue and is the most wearing upon the whole constitution is almost entirely caused by application to the removal of something to be apprehended in the future, or to interests beyond those of the moment, or of the individual; to the laying up of wealth, to the preparation of something, to accomplishing something in the mind of another, and especially to small and petty details which are uninteresting in themselves and which engage the attention at all only because of the bearing they have on some general end of more importance which is seen ahead.

In the interest which natural scenery inspires there is the strongest contrast to this. It is for itself and at the moment it is enjoyed. The attention is aroused and the mind occupied without purpose, without a continuation of the common process of relating the present action, thought or perception to some future end. There is little else that has this quality so purely. There are few enjoyments with which regard for something outside and beyond the enjoyment of the moment can ordinarily be so little mixed. The pleasures of the table are irresistibly associated with the care of hunger and the repair of the bodily waste. In all social pleasures and all pleasures which are usually enjoyed in association with the social pleasure, the care for the opinion of others, or the good of others largely mingles. In the pleasures of literature, the laying up of ideas and self-improvement are purposes which cannot be kept out of view. This, however, is in very slight degree, if at all, the case with the enjoyment of the emotions caused by natural scenery. It therefore results that the enjoyment of scenery employs the mind without fatigue and yet exercises it, tranquilizes it and yet enlivens it; and thus, through the influence of the mind over the body, gives the effect of refreshing rest and reinvigoration to the whole system.

Men who are rich enough and who are sufficiently free from anxiety with regard to their wealth can and do provide places of this needed recreation for themselves. They have done so from the earliest periods known in the history of the world, for the great men of the Babylonians, the Persians and the Hebrews, had their rural retreats, as large and as luxurious as those of the aristocracy of Europe at present. There are in the islands of Great Britain and Ireland more than one thousand private parks and notable grounds devoted to luxury and recreation. The value of these grounds amounts to many millions of dollars and the cost of their annual maintenance is greater than that of the national schools; their only advantage to the commonwealth is obtained through the recreation they afford to their owners (except as these extend hospitality to others) and these owners with their families number less than one in six thousand of the whole population.

The enjoyment of the choicest natural scenes in the country and the means of recreation connected with them is thus a monopoly, in a very peculiar manner, of a very few, very rich people. The great mass of society, including those to whom it would be of the greatest benefit, is excluded from it. In the nature of the case private parks can never be used by the mass of the people in any country nor by any considerable number even of the rich, except by the favor of a few, and in dependence on them.

Thus without means are taken by government to withhold them from the grasp of individuals, all places favorable in scenery to the recreation of the mind and body will be closed against the great body of the people. For the same reason that the water of rivers should be guarded against private appropriation and the use of it for the purpose of navigation and otherwise protected against obstructions, portions of natural scenery may therefore properly be guarded and cared for by government. To simply reserve them from monopoly by individuals, however, it will be obvious, is not all that is necessary. It is necessary that they should be laid open to the use of the body of the people.

The establishment by government of great public grounds for the free enjoyment of the people under certain circumstances, is thus justified and enforced as a political duty.

Such a provision, however, having regard to the whole people of a State, has never before been made and the reason it has not is evident.

It has always been the conviction of the governing classes of the old world that it is necessary that the large mass of all human communities should spend their lives in almost constant labor and that the power of enjoying beauty either of nature or of art in any high degree, requires a cultivation of certain faculties, which is impossible to these humble toilers. Hence it is thought better, so far as the recreations of the masses of a nation receive attention from their rulers, to provide artificial pleasures for them, such as theatres, parades, and promenades where they will be amused by the equipages of the rich and the animation of crowds.

It is unquestionably true that excessive and persistent devotion to sordid interests cramp and distort the power of appreciating natural beauty and destroy the love of it which the Almighty has implanted in every human being, and which is so intimately and mysteriously associated with the moral perceptions and intuitions, but it is not true that exemption from toil, much leisure, much study, much wealth are necessary to the exercise of the esthetic and contemplative faculties. It is the folly of laws which have permitted and favored the monopoly by privileged classes of many of the means supplied in nature for the gratification, exercise and education of the esthetic faculties that has caused the appearance of dullness and weakness and disease of these faculties in the mass of the subjects of kings. And it is against a limitation of the means of such education to the rich that the wise legislation of free governments must be directed. By such legislation the anticipation of the revered Downing may be realized.

The dread of the ignorant exclusive, who has no faith in the refinement of a republic, will stand abashed in the next century, before a whole people whose system of voluntary education embraces (combined with perfect individual freedom), not only common schools of rudimentary knowledge, but common enjoyments for all classes in the higher realms of art, letters, science, social recreations and enjoyments. Were our legislators but wise enough to understand, today, the destinies of the New World, the gentility of Sir Philip Sidney, made universal, would be not half so much a miracle fifty years hence in America, as the idea of a whole nation of laboring men reading and writing, was, in his day, in England.

It was in accordance with these views of the destiny of the New World and the duty of a Republican Government that Congress enacted that the Yosemite should be held, guarded and managed for the free use of the whole body of the people forever, and that the care of it, and the hospitality of admitting strangers from all parts of the world to visit it and enjoy it freely, should be a duty of dignity and be committed only to a sovereign State.

The trust having been accepted, it will be the duty of the legislature to define the responsibilities, the rights and the powers of the Commissioners, whom by the Act of Congress, it will be the duty of the Executive of the State to appoint. These must be determined by a consideration of the purposes to which the ground is to be devoted and must be simply commensurate with those purposes.

The main duty with which the Commissioners should be charged should be to give every advantage practicable to the mass of the people to benefit by that which is peculiar to this ground and which has caused

Congress to treat it differently from other parts of the public domain. This peculiarity consists wholly in its natural scenery.

The first point to be kept in mind then is the preservation and maintenance as exactly as is possible of the natural scenery; the restriction, that is to say, within the narrowest limits consistent with the necessary accommodation of visitors, of all artificial constructions and the prevention of all constructions markedly inharmonious with the scenery or which would unnecessarily obscure, distort or detract from the dignity of the scenery.

In addition to the more immediate and obvious arrangements by which this duty is enforced, there are two considerations which should not escape attention.

First; the value of the district in its present condition as a museum of natural science and the danger — indeed the certainty — that without care many of the species of plants now flourishing upon it will be lost and many interesting objects be defaced or obscured if not destroyed. To illustrate these dangers, it may be stated that numbers of the native plants of large districts of the Atlantic States have almost wholly disappeared and that most of the common weeds of the farms are of foreign origin, having choked out the native vegetation. Many of the finer specimens of the most important tree in the scenery of the Yosemite have been already destroyed and the proclamation of the Governor, issued after the passage of the Act of Congress, forbidding the destruction of trees in the district, alone prevented the establishment of a saw mill within it. Notwithstanding the proclamation many fine trees have been felled and others girdled within the year. Indians and others have set fire to the forests and herbage and numbers of trees have been killed by these fires; the giant tree before referred to as probably the noblest tree now standing on the earth has been burned completely through the bark near the ground for a distance of more than one hundred feet of its circumference; not only have trees been cut, hacked, barked and fired in prominent positions, but rocks in the midst of the most picturesque natural scenery have been broken, painted and discolored, by fires built against them. In travelling to the Yosemite and within a few miles of the nearest point at which it can be approached by a wheeled vehicle, the Commissioners saw other picturesque rocks stencilled over with advertisements of patent medicines and found the walls of the Bower Cave, one of the most beautiful natural objects in the State, already so much broken and scratched by thoughtless visitors that it is evident that unless the practice should be prevented not many years will pass before its natural charm will be quite destroyed.

Second; it is important that it should be remembered that in permitting the sacrifice of anything that would be of the slightest value to future visitors to the convenience, bad taste, playfulness, carelessness, or wanton destructiveness of present visitors, we probably yield in each case the interest of uncounted millions to the selfishness of a few individuals. It is an important fact that as civilization advances, the interest of men in natural scenes of sublimity and beauty increases. Where a century ago one traveller came to enjoy the scenery of the

Alps, thousands come now and where even forty years ago one small inn accommodated the visitors to the White Hills of New Hampshire, half a dozen grand hotels, each accommodating hundreds are now overcrowded every Summer. In the early part of the present century the summer visitors to the Highlands of Scotland did not give business enough to support a single inn, a single stage coach or a single guide. They now give business to several Rail Road trains, scores of steamboats and thousands of men and horses every day. It is but sixteen years since the Yosemite was first seen by a white man, several visitors have since made a journey of several thousand miles at large cost to see it, and notwithstanding the difficulties which now interpose, hundreds resort to it annually. Before many years, if proper facilities are offered, these hundreds will become thousands and in a century the whole number of visitors will be counted by millions. An injury to the scenery so slight that it may be unheeded by any visitor now, will be one multiplied by these millions. But again, the slight harm which the few hundred visitors of this year might do, if no care were taken to prevent it, would not be slight, if it should be repeated by millions. At some time, therefore, laws to prevent an unjust use by individuals of that which is not individual but public property, must be made and rigidly enforced. The principle of justice involved is the same now that it will be then; such laws as this principle demands will be more easily enforced, and there will be less hardship in their action, if the abuses they are designed to prevent are never allowed to become customary but are checked while they are yet of unimportant consequence. It should, then, be made the duty of the Commission to prevent a wanton or careless disregard on the part of anyone entering the Yosemite or the Grove, of the rights of posterity as well as of cotemporary visitors, and the Commission should be clothed with proper authority and given the necessary means for this purpose.

This duty of preservation is the first which falls upon the State under the Act of Congress, because the millions who are hereafter to benefit by the Act have the largest interest in it, and the largest interest should be first and most strenuously guarded.

Next to this, and for a similar reason preceding all other duties of the State in regard to this trust, is that of aiding to make this appropriation of Congress available as soon and as generally as may be economically practicable to those whom it is designed to benefit. Had Congress not thought best to depart from the usual method of dealing with the public lands in this case, it would have been practicable for one man to have bought the whole, to have appropriated it wholly to his individual pleasure or to have refused admittance to any who were unable to pay a certain price as admission fee, or as a charge for the entertainment which he would have had a monopoly of supplying. The result would have been a rich man's park, and for the present, so far as the great body of the people are concerned, it is, and as long as the present arrangements continue, it will remain, practically, the property only of the rich.

A man travelling from Stockton to the Yosemite or the Mariposa Grove is commonly three or four days on the road at an expense of from thirty to forty dollars, and arrives in the majority of cases quite overcome with the fatigue and unaccustomed hardships of the journey. Few persons, especially few women, are able to enjoy or profit by the scenery and air for days afterwards. Meantime they remain at an expense of from $3 to $12 per day for themselves, their guide and horses, and many leave before they have recovered from their first exhaustion and return home jaded and ill. The distance is not over one hundred miles, and with such roads and public conveyances as are found elsewhere in the State the trip might be made easily and comfortably in one day and at a cost of ten or twelve dollars. With similar facilities of transportation, the provisions and all the necessities of camping could also be supplied at moderate rates. To realize the advantages which are offered the people of the State in this gift of the Nation, therefor, the first necessity is a road from the termination of the present roads leading towards the district. At present there is no communication with it except by means of a very poor trail for a distance of nearly forty miles from the Yo Semite and twenty from the Mariposa Grove.

Besides the advantages which such a road would have in reducing the expense, time and fatigue of a visit to the tract to the whole public at once, it would also serve the important purpose of making it practicable to convey timber and other articles necessary for the accommodation of visitors into the Yo Semite from without, and thus the necessity, or the temptation, to cut down its groves and to prepare its surface for tillage would be avoided. Until a road is made it must be very difficult to prevent this. The Commissioners propose also in laying out a road to the Mariposa Grove that it shall be carried completely around it, so as to offer a barrier of bare ground to the approach of fires, which nearly every year sweep upon it from the adjoining country, and which during the last year alone have caused injuries, exemption from which it will be thought before many years would have been cheaply obtained at ten times the cost of the road.

Within the Yosemite the Commissioners propose to cause to be constructed a double trail, which, on the completion of our approach road, may be easily made suitable for the passage of a single vehicle, and which shall enable visitors to make a complete circuit of all the broader parts of the valley and to cross the meadows at certain points, reaching all the finer points of view to which it can be carried without great expense. When carriages are introduced it is proposed that they shall be driven for the most part up one side and down the other of the valley, suitable resting places and turnouts for passing being provided at frequent intervals. The object of this arrangement is to reduce the necessity for artificial construction within the narrowest practicable limits, destroying as it must the natural conditions of the ground and presenting an unpleasant object to the eye in the midst of the scenery. The trail or narrow road could also be kept more in the shade, could take a more picturesque course, would be less dusty, and could be much more cheaply kept in repair. From this trail a few paths would also need to be formed, leading to points of view which would only be accessible to persons on foot. Several small bridges would also be required.

The Commission also propose the construction of five cabins at points in the valley conveniently near to those most frequented by visitors, especially near the foot of the cascades, but at the same time near to convenient camping places. These cabins would be let to tenants with the condition that they should have constantly open one comfortable room as a free resting place for visitors, with the proper private accommodations for women, and that they should keep constantly on hand in another room a supply of certain simple necessities for camping parties, including tents, cooking utensils and provisions; the tents and utensils to be let, and the provisions to be sold at rates to be limited by the terms of the contract.

The Commissioners ask and recommend that sums be appropriated for these and other purposes named below as follows:

For the expense already incurred in the survey and transfer of the Yosemite and Mariposa Big Tree Grove from the United States to the State of California .... $ 2,000.
For the construction of 30 miles more or less of double trail & foot paths .... 3,000.
For the construction of Bridges .... 1,600.
For the construction and finishing five cabins, closets, stairways, railings &c .... 2,000.
Salary of Superintendent (2 years) .... 2,400.
For surveys, advertising, & incidentals .... 1,000.
For aid in the construction of a road .... 25,000.

$ 37,000.

The Commissioners trust that after this amount shall have been expended the further necessary expenses for the management of the domain will be defrayed by the proceeds of rents and licenses which will be collected upon it.

The Yosemite yet remains to be considered as a field of study for science and art. Already students of science and artists have been attracted to it from the Atlantic States and a number of artists have at heavy expense spent the Summer in sketching the scenery. That legislation should, when practicable within certain limits, give encouragement to the pursuit of science and art has been fully recognized as a duty by this State. The pursuit of science and of art, while it tends more than any other human pursuit to the benefit of the commonwealth and the advancement of civilization, does not correspondingly put money into the hands of the pursuers. Their means are generally extremely limited. They are likely by the nature of their studies to be the best counsellors which can be had in respect to certain of the duties which will fall upon the proposed Commission, and it is right that they should if possible be honorably represented in the constitution of the Commission.

Congress has provided that the Executive shall appoint eight Commissioners, and that they shall give their services gratuitously. It is but just that the State should defray the travelling expenses necessarily incurred in the discharge of their duty. It is proposed that the allowance for this purpose shall be limited in amount to four hundred dollars per annum, for each

Commissioner, or so much thereof as shall have been actually expended in travelling to and from the ground and while upon it. It is also proposed that of the eight Commissioners to be appointed by the Executive, four shall be appointed annually and that these four shall be students of Natural Science or Landscape Artists. It is advised also that in order that it may be in the power of the Governor when he sees fit to offer the slight consideration represented in the sum of $400 proposed to be allowed each Commissioner for travelling expenses as an inducement to men of scientific note and zealous artists to visit the State, that he shall not necessarily be restricted in these appointments to citizens of the State. The Yosemite being a trust from the whole nation, it seems eminently proper that so much liberality in its management should be authorized.

A Note on the Text

The text of this report is taken from a manuscript in the Frederick Law Olmsted Papers in the Manuscript Division of the Library of Congress, Washington, D.C. It was found in 1952 at the office of the Olmsted Brothers firm in Brookline, Massachusetts. Written in ink in the hand of Henry Perkins, Olmsted's secretary in California, it is entitled "Preliminary Report upon the Yosemite and Big Tree Grove." Presumably, this is the text that Olmsted used when he read his report to the Yosemite Commission in 1865.

Pages 5 through 14 are missing from the 52-page manuscript. It appears that Olmsted removed those pages to use in a letter to the editor of the *New York Evening Post* that was published on June 18, 1868. Signed "F. L.O.," the letter describes the scenery of the Yosemite area, and its last lines duplicate the first lines of page 15 of the manuscript. Olmsted's biographer, Laura Wood Roper, first combined the two texts and published them in the October, 1952, issue of *Landscape Architecture.*

Several alterations and corrections appear in pencil on the Henry Perkins manuscript. It is unclear whether it was Olmsted or Perkins who made the changes, although at least two corrections are surely Olmsted's doing. With only two exceptions, the alterations correct a grammatical mistake or substitute the proper word for one that was written in error. Because they do not affect the meaning of the text, those changes have been incorporated in the text printed here.

This form of the Preliminary Report appears with notes and additional background material in *The Papers of Frederick Law Olmsted, Volume Five: The California Years, 1863-1865*, Victoria Post Ranney, editor, pages 488-516.

SELECTED BIBLIOGRAPHY

BREWER, WILLIAM H. *Up and Down California in 1860-64; The Journal of William H. Brewer.* Edited by Francis P. Farquhar. New Haven: Yale University Press, 1930.

ERRINGTON, HARRIET. "Harriet Errington's Letters and Journal from California, 1864-1865." Typescript. Yosemite Research Library, Yosemite National Park, California.

HUTH, HANS. "Yosemite, the Story of an Idea." *Sierra Club Bulletin* 33 (March 1948): 65.

JOHNSON, ROBERT UNDERWOOD. "Amateur Management of the Yosemite Scenery." *The Century* 40 (Sept. 1890): 797-98.

JONES, HOLWAY R. *John Muir and the Sierra Club; The Battle for Yosemite.* San Francisco: Sierra Club, 1965.

McGUIRE, DIANE KOSTIAL. "Frederick Law Olmsted in California; An Analysis of His Contributions to Landscape Architecture and City Planning." Master's thesis, University of California, Berkeley, 1956.

NASH, RODERICK. *Wilderness and the American Mind*. New Haven: Yale University Press, 1967.

OLMSTED, FREDERICK LAW. *Governmental Preservation of Natural Scenery*. Brookline, Mass.: self-published, 1890.

—. *The Papers of Frederick Law Olmsted, Volume V, The California Frontier, 1863-1865*. Victoria Post Ranney, editor. Baltimore and London: The Johns Hopkins University Press, 1990.

—. "The Yosemite Valley and the Mariposa Big Trees: A Preliminary Report, 1865." Reproduced with a foreword by Laura Wood Roper. *Landscape Architecture 43* (October 1952): 12-25.

ROPER, LAURA WOOD. *FLO: A Biography of Frederick Law Olmsted*. Baltimore and London: The Johns Hopkins University Press, 1973.

RUNTE, ALFRED. *National Parks: The American Experience*. Lincoln and London: University of Nebraska Press, 1979.

—. *Yosemite, The Embattled Wilderness*. Lincoln and London: University of Nebraska Press, 1990.

STEVENSON, ELIZABETH. *Park Maker: A Life of Frederick Law Olmsted*. New York: Macmillan Publishing Co., 1977.

**YOSEMITE
ASSOCIATION**

The Yosemite Association is a 501(c)(3) non-profit membership organization; since 1923, it has initiated and supported a variety of interpretive, educational, research, scientific, and environmental programs in Yosemite National Park, in cooperation with the National Park Service. Revenue generated by its publishing program, park visitor center bookstores, Yosemite Outdoor Adventures, membership dues, and donations enables it to provide services and direct financial support that promote park stewardship and enrich the visitor experience. To learn more about the association's activities and other publications, or for information about membership, please write to the Yosemite Association, P.O. Box 230, El Portal, CA 95318, call (209) 379-2646, or visit www.yosemite.org.